Book #3 of 3 in the Bipol

Ethel and Ruthie

Dust Bowl Flashback: Ethel's Great Chicken-Powered Exodus

Prologue:

The year was 1935, and the Oklahoma sky had turned its back on the earth. Dust storms rolled in like angry gods, black blizzards that swallowed the sun and left farms looking like the surface of the moon after a tantrum. Eighteen-year-old Ethel May Jenkins—gangly, red-headed, and already convinced the world was one big puzzle waiting for her to solve it—stood on the sagging porch of the family farmhouse and watched another horizon disappear.

Inside, her pa was coughing up Oklahoma, one lungful at a time. Her ma was packing what little hadn't blown away. And

Ethel? Ethel was staring at the broken Conestoga wagon in the side yard, wheels half-buried in drift dirt, and thinking: That thing's got potential.

Most folks were lining up for California handouts. Ethel figured if she was going to migrate, she'd do it with style. Or at least with chickens.

She spent three feverish days in the barn, hammering and wiring and muttering to herself in the way that made neighbors whisper "tetched." Her autism turned the chaos into music: every nail, every gear ratio, every squawk from the henhouse fit into a pattern only she could see. By the end, she'd transformed the wagon into something that looked like a prairie schooner had mated with a Rube Goldberg fever dream.

The axle was reinforced with scavenged Ford parts. A sail—made from her mother's best bedsheets—was rigged to catch whatever wind dared show up. And the motive power? Thirty-seven highly offended Rhode Island Red hens, harnessed in rotating shifts to a treadmill system that turned the wagon wheels. Ethel called it the Cluck-O-Mobile. Her father called it blasphemy. The chickens just called it Tuesday.

Departure day arrived with a sky the color of dried blood. The Jenkins family watched from the porch as Ethel climbed aboard in overalls two sizes too big, a straw hat tied under her chin with baling twine, and a harmonica in her pocket for "aerodynamic testing."

Pa handed her a mason jar of water and a warning: "Girl, you're fixin' to die in a ditch."

Ethel grinned the grin that would one day terrorize Vancouver Island. "Only if the ditch is interestin'."

She cracked a makeshift rein—really just a length of rope tied to the lead hen's leg—and hollered, "Mush, you feathered ingrates!"

The Cluck-O-Mobile lurched forward with all the grace of a drunk buffalo. Chickens flapped, squawked, and ran for their lives on the treadmill. The wagon wheels turned. Slowly. Painfully. But they turned.

Half a mile down the road, a dust devil spun up as if it had taken a personal offense. Ethel yanked a lever. The bedsheet sail billowed wildly. The wagon veered sharply, chickens screeching in unison, and the dust devil missed them by ten feet. Ethel whooped so loud it echoed across the empty fields.

Word spread faster than the dust. By the time she reached the Texas panhandle, people lined the road to watch the red-headed girl in the chicken wagon. Some laughed. Some threw rocks. Most just stared, because in a world falling apart, Ethel Jenkins was building something ridiculous and making it work.

In Amarillo, a trucker hauling empty crates to California took pity—or maybe he just wanted the story. He offered to tow the Cluck-O-Mobile for fifty miles if Ethel would let him ride along and "see the contraption up close." Ethel negotiated: tow for a hundred miles, plus he had to let her install a chicken-powered horn on his truck. Deal struck.

The horn—a series of tin cans and pulleys that produced a sound like a goose being strangled—worked exactly once before the trucker ripped it off and threatened to leave her in the desert. Ethel just laughed, re-harnessed her hens, and carried on.

Somewhere in New Mexico, a sheriff pulled her over for "operating an unlicensed poultry vehicle." Ethel played "Oh! Susanna" on her harmonica until he begged her to stop. She left town with a police escort for three miles and a stolen deputy's wristwatch (purely for "timing the hen rotation efficiency," she claimed).

By the time she crossed into British Columbia months later—wagon battered, chickens down to twenty-three battle-hardened survivors, and Ethel herself sunburned, dust-caked, and triumphant—she'd turned a desperate escape into legend.

At the Canadian border, the customs officer asked what she was declaring. Ethel swept an arm toward the wagon. "One mobile henhouse, twenty-three units of premium poultry propulsion, and a lifetime supply of gumption."

The officer stamped her papers without saying a word. Probably figured anyone crazy enough to cross a continent powered by chickens deserved whatever was coming. Years later, telling the story to wide-eyed grandchildren around a driftwood fire on Chesterman Beach, Ethel would always end the same way:

"I didn't run from the Dust Bowl, darlin's. I out-chickened it."

And then she'd wink, pull out that same battered harmonica, and play a few off-key notes while the Pacific rain drummed approval on the cabin roof.

Chapter 1: The Holographic Haunting

The rain on Vancouver Island doesn't fall so much as it loiters, hanging in the air like it's got nowhere better to be. On the day of Ethel Hargrove's "un-funeral," it was doing its usual impression of a wet sheepdog—damp, persistent, and mildly judgmental.

Beatrice Hargrove—Bea to anyone who didn't want a frosty glare—stood under the dripping eaves of her mother's cedar-shingled cabin, clutching a manila envelope as if it might bite her. At sixty-two, Bea had the posture of a woman who'd spent forty years shushing teenagers in a library and had finally retired only to find that silence was overrated.

Inside the cabin, the rest of the family milled about in various stages of soggy grief and hunger. Finn, her thirty-four-year-old son, was poking at a gadget on the coffee table with the intensity of a bomb tech. Lila, twenty-eight and perpetually windswept, was arranging wildflowers in a chipped coffee mug while humming something that sounded suspiciously like a sea shanty. Uncle Zeke, ninety-one going on twelve, sat in Ethel's ancient rocking chair, regaling Cousin Marla—who'd flown in from Vancouver looking like she'd been personally offended by the ferry—with tales of Dust Bowl tornadoes that could suck the chrome off a trailer hitch.

Bea cleared her throat. Twice. The third time, she added a sharp "Ahem" that could slice bread.

"Mother left specific instructions," she announced, holding up the envelope. "No church. No tears. Tacos mandatory."

Lila whooped. Finn didn't look up. Zeke nodded solemnly, as if tacos were a sacred ceremony.

Bea slit the envelope with the precision of a surgeon. Inside was a single flash drive labeled in Ethel's spidery handwriting: PLAY ME FIRST, YA GOOBS.

Finn's head snapped up. "Is that… holographic tech? Grandma was working on something like this before—" He stopped, suddenly remembering they weren't supposed to be sad.

Bea handed him the drive as if it were radioactive. Finn plugged it into the old projector Ethel had bolted to the ceiling beams years ago "for movie nights," although no one could remember her ever watching a film without making louder commentary than the dialogue.

The lights dimmed on their own. A low hum filled the room. Then, in the center of the rug, a life-sized image flickered into existence.

Ethel Hargrove stood there in her favorite denim overalls, hair in twin gray braids, eyes twinkling as if she'd just rigged the projector to explode (which, knowing Ethel, wasn't impossible). She looked exactly as she had the day she'd keeled over in her workshop—mid-laugh, mid-sentence, mid-mischief.

"Howdy, ya sorry bunch of wet chickens," holographic Ethel drawled, Oklahoma accent thick as blackstrap molasses. "If yer watchin' this, I've finally kicked the bucket. Good riddance to gravity, I say."

Lila let out a happy squeak. Zeke slapped his knee. Marla pulled back as if someone had offered her a live eel.

Ethel's hologram paced, boots not quite touching the floor. "Now, I ain't leavin' y'all a pile of money, 'cause money's boring and y'all would just fight over it. Instead, I'm leavin' you my greatest invention yet: the Ethel Challenges. Complete 'em all, and you get the real inheritance. Fail, and... well, I'll haunt you with bad banjo music."

Finn whispered, "She reverse-engineered volumetric projection from a 3D printer and a busted Kinect. This is genius."

Bea pinched the bridge of her nose. "Mother, this is undignified."

Hologram Ethel cupped a hand to her ear. "What's that, Beatrice? Can't hear you over the sound of FUN." She grinned. "First challenge starts... now!"

The projector whirred. A burst of virtual confetti exploded from Ethel's outstretched hands—except the confetti was real. Somehow. Glitter, streamers, and what appeared to be shredded bingo cards shot into the room like a party cannon.

Zeke, caught mid-rock, toppled backward out of the chair and rolled straight through the open door into the mud puddle on the porch with a magnificent sploosh.

Lila doubled over laughing. Finn tried to catch the falling projector remote and succeeded only in knocking over a lamp. Marla shrieked as glitter settled in her perfectly highlighted hair like obscene dandruff.

Hologram Ethel winked out with a final cackle: "Welcome home, family. Try not to drown."

Bea stared at the chaos, rain dripping from the doorway, her brother-in-law flailing in mud, her children howling with laughter.

For the first time in years, she felt something dangerously close to a smile tugging at her lips.

"Mornin', ya bunch of soggy socks," she drawled. "Hope y'all slept off the taco coma. Challenge Two: Time for a treasure hunt. I hid my Okie Artifacts all over this drippy island—little pieces of home to remind you where you came from. First clue: Head to the place where the goats wear sweaters and the hippies smell like patchouli and regret."

Lila, already halfway through her second mug of nettle tea, shot up so fast she knocked over her chair. "Coombs! The goats-on-the-roof market! That's totally it!"

Chapter 2: Dust Bowl Detours and Island Idiocy

The morning after the holographic confetti ambush, the rain had settled into a half-hearted drizzle, the kind that couldn't decide whether to commit or just threaten. Inside Ethel's cabin, the air smelled of stale tacos, wet cedar, and the faint ozone tang of whatever wizardry powered her projector.

At exactly 9:00 a.m.—because Ethel Hargrove had never been late for chaos in her life—the projector hummed again. The family, bleary-eyed and nursing coffee in mismatched mugs, gathered around the kitchen table like survivors of a very small, very glittery war.

Hologram Ethel flickered into view above the table, this time wearing a battered straw sombrero she'd definitely stolen from a tourist in 1972. She held a mason jar that sloshed suspiciously.

Finn blinked. "Grandma hid something at a tourist trap famous for goat merchandise?"

Bea pinched the bridge of her nose hard enough to leave marks. "We are not driving an hour each way to chase barnyard animals for Mother's sentimental junk."

But twenty minutes later, they were doing exactly that.

The family van—an ancient rust-colored Volkswagen Westfalia that Ethel had nicknamed "The Damp Slug"—wheezed to life with a cough and a prayer. Bea drove, white-knuckled. Finn rode in the passenger seat, tablet balanced on his knees, trying to reverse-engineer the hologram app. Lila and Zeke shared the middle bench, while Marla—still offended by the entire province—perched on the back bench looking like she'd rather be anywhere else.

As they wound along the Pacific Rim Highway, Zeke launched into storyteller mode.

"Your grandma was eighteen when she left Oklahoma," he began, voice cracking with age and mischief. "Skinny little thing with freckles like cinnamon on milk. Dust Bowl had eaten the farm whole. Pa was sick, Ma was prayin', and Ethel? Ethel was in the barn buildin' a wagon powered by chickens."

Lila leaned forward. "The Cluck-O-Mobile. Tell it right, Uncle Zeke."

Zeke grinned, missing teeth and all. "She took that broke-down Conestoga, slapped on some Model T axles, rigged a sail outta Ma's best bedsheets, and harnessed thirty-seven hens to a treadmill. Called it 'poultry propulsion.' Cranked a handle, chickens ran like the devil was chasin' 'em, wheels turned. Slow as Christmas, but it moved."

Bea glanced in the rearview mirror. "She left in a dust storm so thick you couldn't see your hand in front of your face. Pa said she'd die in a ditch."

Zeke cackled. "She just yelled back, 'Only if the ditch is interestin'!' and off she went. Played that harmonica the whole way—said it confused the twisters into missin' her."

Finn looked up from his tablet. "Crowdsourced migration with aggressive poultry. Iconic."

They reached Coombs just as the morning tour buses were unloading. The sod roof of the Old Country Market was dotted with goats in tiny knitted sweaters, munching grass and judging humanity. Tourists milled below, buying goat-shaped soap and overpriced fudge.

Ethel's clue had specified "the goat with the aristocratic name." They found him near the far end: a smug brown-and-white billy wearing a red cardigan embroidered with SIR BAAART.

Tucked beneath the cardigan, secured with baling twine, was a small rusted tin box.

Lila reached up—standing on tiptoes—and liberated it while Sir Baaart chewed her sleeve in mild protest.

Inside the box: a battered harmonica, green with age, and a folded note in Ethel's unmistakable scrawl.

Artifact One: The Mouth Organ of Destiny.

Played this from Okla-freakin'-homa to BC to keep the devils away—dust devils, border guards, lonely nights, you name it. Didn't always work, but it annoyed 'em somethin' fierce.

Next clue tomorrow at dawn. Now git before the tourists start takin' pictures of your behinds.

Lila immediately put the harmonica to her lips and blew an experimental note. It sounded like a goose being stepped on in a tin bathtub. A nearby toddler burst into tears. A goat bleated in harmony.

On the drive home, the road was slick with rain. Lila, undeterred, kept practicing. A particularly enthusiastic wheeze sent the harmonica flying from her hands. It bounced off Finn's head, ricocheted off the dashboard, and landed squarely in Bea's lap.

Bea startled, jerked the wheel. The van fishtailed toward a ditch lined with blackberry brambles.

Screams filled the air. Zeke yelled, "Tornado drill!" and dove for the floorboards, taking Marla's designer purse with him.

Bea wrestled the van back onto the pavement, heart hammering, and pulled over onto the gravel shoulder. Rain pattered on the roof like impatient fingers.

Silence fell, broken only by the tick of cooling engine and distant surf.

Bea stared at the harmonica in her lap. Then, slowly, deliberately, she raised it to her mouth and blew a single clear note—wobbly, off-key, but unmistakably deliberate.

The van went still.

Bea lowered the instrument, cheeks flushed beneath her practical bob. "Your grandmother always said the only thing that ever shut Uncle Zeke up was music."

Zeke, still on the floor, peered up with a grin. "Hot damn, Bea. You got the gift."

Marla, disentangling her purse strap from Zeke's boot, muttered something about therapy.

But no one argued when Bea slipped the harmonica into her coat pocket.

The rest of the drive was quiet, punctuated only by the swish of wipers and the occasional goat-scented burp from the back seat. Outside, the rainforest pressed close, dripping and ancient.

And for the first time since arriving on the island, Bea found herself humming—softly, tentatively—under her breath.

An old Okie tune Ethel used to play on long rainy nights when the power went out, and the only light came from the woodstove.

It didn't sound half bad.

Chapter 3: Gadget Mayhem in the Mist

Dawn on Chesterman Beach is a moody masterpiece: pewter sky, gunmetal waves, and mist so thick it feels like the ocean is exhaling directly onto the sand. The Hargroves arrived looking like a mismatched expedition—Bea in a sensible rain jacket the color of wet asphalt, Finn bundled in a hoodie two sizes too big, Lila in tie-dye leggings and mismatched rubber boots, Zeke wrapped in a blanket that smelled faintly of mothballs and campfire, and Marla trailing behind in pristine white linen because apparently no one had told her this was a mud-optional event.

They parked the Damp Slug at the trailhead and trudged down the beach, following Ethel's third clue: "Dig where the rain tried to kill me but only made me stronger. Bring shovels and a sense of humor—y'all gonna need both."

Finn, consulting his phone, pointed toward a cluster of massive driftwood logs. "Grandma's old workshop lean-to collapsed in the '98 storm. She rebuilt it into something she called the Rain Repeller. Bet that's the spot."

They found it half-buried under a dune of sand and kelp: a battered metal lockbox stenciled with faded letters—E.H. PROPERTY OF DO NOT TOUCH UNLESS YOU WANT A SURPRISE.

Lila pried it open with a driftwood stick. Inside, nestled in oilcloth, was the contraption itself: a Frankenstein marriage of satellite dish, patio umbrella frame, leaf blower, and what looked suspiciously like parts from a 1950s vacuum cleaner. A hand-painted label read: RAIN REPELLER MK III – NOW WITH 30% LESS FLOODING (RESULTS MAY VARY).

The moment Finn lifted it out, the air shimmered. Hologram Ethel popped into existence right on the sand, wearing yellow rubber boots, a clear plastic rain cape, and an expression of pure devilment.

"Well, butter my butt and call me a biscuit!" she crowed. "Look at y'all, showin' up early for once. Challenge Three: Activate the Rain Repeller. It'll keep you dry as a bone in a monsoon. Mostly. Probably. Don't quote me."

Bea folded her arms. "Define 'mostly.'"

Ethel's hologram leaned in conspiratorially. "Beatrice, honey, if I wanted certainty I'd have become an accountant. Where's the fun in that?"

Marla sniffed. "This is absurd. We're standing on a beach in January holding a junkyard umbrella. I have a spa appointment in Victoria tomorrow."

Zeke chuckled. "Girl, the only thing gettin' massaged tomorrow is your ego when this thing works."

Lila, never one to wait for consensus, flipped the large red toggle switch labeled ON (DUH).

The Repeller hummed like an asthmatic cat. A faint blue dome shimmered into existence above their heads, pushing the mist aside in a perfect ten-foot circle. For one glorious moment, they stood in a pocket of dry air while rain hissed down inches away.

Finn's eyes went wide. "Force-field tech from scavenged parts. Grandma was a chaotic engineer god."

Then the humming turned into a gurgle.

Then a groan.

Then—WHOOSH.

The dome inverted. Every droplet it had repelled for the last five minutes came roaring back down in a single, targeted deluge—like the Pacific Ocean had saved up a personal bucket just for them.

Slapstick exploded in glorious slow motion.

Zeke slipped backward on wet kelp and landed butt-first in a tide pool. A dozen tiny crabs immediately staged a protest march across his lap. "Consarn it!" he bellowed. "I'm bein' colonized!"

Finn's tablet shorted with a pathetic spark and a smell of fried silicon. He held it aloft like a dying soldier. "Noooo! My notes on Grandma's projection algorithm!"

Lila tried to bolt for cover and executed a perfect cartoon banana-peel slide, face-planting into a mound of wet sand that squelched up her nose. She came up sputtering, hair plastered like seaweed, laughing so hard she couldn't breathe.

Marla—poor, pristine Marla—caught the brunt of the waterfall. Her white linen went transparent in seconds. She shrieked a note that could shatter crystal, arms flailing, and staggered straight into a pile of bull kelp that wrapped around her ankles like possessive octopus arms. Down she went, landing on her designer rear with a splat that echoed off the drift logs.

Bea stood dead center, unmoving, as the column of water hammered her like judgment day. When it finally stopped, she looked like she'd been pressure-washed. Water streamed off her nose. Her practical bob was now a drowned rat toupee.

Silence fell, broken only by dripping and the distant bark of a sea lion that sounded suspiciously like laughter.

Then hologram Ethel started slow-clapping.

"That's my girls and boys!" she whooped. "First time I tested Mk I, I flooded the neighbor's koi pond. Fish flopping everywhere—like sushi rain. Took me three versions to get it down to only occasional biblical flooding."

Marla, wringing out her scarf like it had personally betrayed her, snarled, "This is assault! I'm suing the estate!"

Ethel leaned toward her. "Sugar, the only thing gettin' sued today is your fashion sense. White after Labor Day on a beach? Rookie mistake."

Zeke, still seated in his crab parliament, pointed a gnarled finger. "Ethel, you evil genius, you planned this, didn't you?"

"'Course I did," Ethel shot back. "Y'all were gettin' too dry behind the ears. Needed a baptism."

Finn, mourning his tablet, muttered, "At least the data's backed up to the cloud."

Lila wiped sand from her mouth. "Cloud. Ha. Very funny, universe."

Bea finally moved. She looked down at the now-silent Repeller in her hands, then at her soaked, giggling, groaning family. Something shifted behind her eyes.

She cleared her throat. "Everybody, back up. We're fixing this thing."

Marla gaped. "You cannot be serious."

"Oh, I'm dead serious," Bea said, rolling up her sleeves with surprising enthusiasm. "Your grandmother was brilliant, but she never met a safety protocol she couldn't ignore. Finn, hand me that multi-tool. Lila, find me wire. Zeke—stop fraternizing with crustaceans and hold this steady."

Zeke saluted with a crab still clinging to his suspenders. "Aye, aye, Captain Soggy!"

Even Marla, muttering about liability, edged closer to watch as Bea—practical, repressed, librarian Bea—began dismantling the control box with driftwood and sheer determination.

Ethel's hologram hovered nearby, arms crossed, grinning like a proud haunt.

"Listen to her," she said softly to no one in particular. "That's my girl. Took seventy years and a small tsunami, but she's rememberin' how to be a Hargrove."

An hour later, after much swearing, one minor electric shock (Zeke volunteered as tribute), and Lila using kelp as impromptu electrical tape, they flipped the switch again.

This time the dome held—steady, gentle, and ringed with a perfect rainbow mist.

The family stood inside it, dry for the first time all morning, staring up in wonder.

Marla touched the edge of the dome gingerly, as if expecting it to bite. "It…it works."

"Mostly," Bea corrected with a small, triumphant smile. "But better."

Ethel gave them a thumbs-up. "That's the spirit. Y'all keep tinkering. Next clue tomorrow—bring your appetite and a change of pants."

She flickered out, leaving only the soft hum of the Repeller and the sound of five very damp Hargroves laughing so hard they had to lean on each other to stay upright.

Even Marla. Especially Marla.

Chesterman Beach at dawn has a beauty that inspires people to write bad poetry. Mist clung to the sand as if it was afraid to let go. Waves hissed secrets to the rocks.

The Hargroves arrived armed with Ethel's third clue: "Dig where the rain tried to kill me but only made me stronger."

Finn translated: "Grandma's old workshop lean-to collapsed in '98. She rebuilt it into the Rain Repeller."

They found the spot—a half-buried metal box near a driftwood log. Inside was a contraption that looked like a satellite dish had mated with an umbrella and a shop vac.

Hologram Ethel appeared the moment Finn touched it, sporting rain boots and a grin sharp enough to cut glass.

Challenge Three: Activate the Rain Repeller. It'll keep you dry as a bone in a downpour. Mostly.

Bea eyed the device. "Define mostly."

Too late. Lila had already flipped the switch.

The Repeller hummed. A dome of air shimmered above them. For ten glorious seconds, the mist parted like the Red Sea.

Then it backfired.

A torrent of captured rainwater blasted downward in a perfect column, drenching everyone inside the "dome" while leaving the surrounding beach untouched. Zeke slipped backward into a tide pool. Crabs objected loudly. Finn's tablet shorted out with a sad pop. Lila tried to run and face-planted in wet sand. Marla—Marla, who'd shown up in white linen, emerged looking like a drowned meringue.

Bea stood in the epicenter, hair plastered to her skull, clothes clinging, holding the now-silent Repeller like a traitor.

Hologram Ethel clapped slowly. "That's my girl. The first time I tested it, I flooded the neighbor's koi pond. Fish everywhere. Like sushi rain."

Bea looked down at herself. Then at her laughing family. Then, slowly, she raised the Repeller like a trophy.

"Again," she said, voice steady. "But this time, we modify it."

Finn's jaw dropped. "Mom?"

Bea was already prying open the control panel with a driftwood stick. "Your grandmother was brilliant, but she never met a safety switch she couldn't ignore. Hand me that wire." Lila whooped and dove to help. Even Marla, wringing out her scarf, edged closer to watch.

By the time the sun burned through the mist an hour later, the Hargroves had a working—mostly—Rain Repeller. It kept a ten-foot circle dry while gently misting a rainbow around the edges.

Hologram Ethel watched them test it, arms crossed, pride shining in her pixelated eyes. "That's the spirit," she said softly. "Y'all are startin' to remember how to be Hargroves."

Then she vanished, leaving only the smell of wet cedar and the sound of a family laughing so hard they didn't care they were soaked to the bone.

=====

Chapter 4: Family Feuds and Feral Fiascos

The fourth hologram arrived at the ungodly hour of 7:00 a.m., because Ethel believed sleep was for people who lacked ambition and caffeine. The projector whirred to life while the family was still fumbling with coffee and yesterday's damp clothes.

Ethel appeared in full Dust Bowl regalia: overalls patched with floral feed-sack fabric, a kerchief tied bandit-style over her mouth, and goggles made from jar lids and electrical tape.

"Rise and shine, ya lazy lumps!" she barked. "Challenge Four: Re-enactment time. Y'all are gonna stage my famous Okie Escape through the rainforest. I left a trail of props from the

Mackenzie Beach parking lot to the big nurse log that looks like a dragon's spine. Follow the twine. Act it out. Bonus points for drama, extra bonus if somebody screams like a banshee."

Bea, mid-sip of black coffee, lowered her mug slowly. "We are not playing dress-up in the woods."

Ethel leaned forward until her pixelated nose almost touched Bea's real one. "Beatrice, darlin', the day you stop playin' dress-up is the day they nail the lid on your coffin. Now move your sensible buttocks." Marla, wrapped in a hotel bathrobe because her linen still hadn't recovered, snorted. "This is ridiculous. I didn't fly first-class to prance around like Okies in mud."

Zeke winked at her. "Honey, the mud's free. Better than your fancy spa—exfoliates and humiliates at the same time."

Finn was already lacing his sneakers. "Think of it as immersive theater with a side of cardio."

Lila clapped. "I call dibs on being young Grandma Ethel!"

Bea sighed the sigh of the eternally resigned and reached for her rain jacket. "Fine. But if anyone twists an ankle, I'm not carrying you."

An hour later, they stood at the trailhead, armed with a ball of orange baling twine Ethel had apparently strung through the rainforest like deranged Christmas lights. Props were stashed at intervals: a miniature wagon wheel, a fake chicken (taxidermied, naturally), a bedsheet sail, and several signs in Ethel's handwriting that read things like DUST DEVIL CROSSING—PANIC OPTIONAL.

Lila launched into character immediately, adopting Ethel's drawl with alarming accuracy. "Onward, ya feathered freeloaders! California or bust—by way of Canada, 'cause I heard the rain's free!"

She cracked an imaginary whip. Zeke, assigned the role of "grumpy hen," flapped his arms and clucked indignantly.

Finn filmed everything on his backup phone, narrating like David Attenborough. "Observe the wild Hargrove in its natural habitat: caffeine-deprived and mildly feral."

They'd made it about half a mile when the trail narrowed and the mud deepened. Bea, bringing up the rear, stepped on a root slick with moss. Her foot shot forward. Arms pinwheeled. She landed flat on her back in a patch of salmonberries with a sound like a wet sack of library books hitting the floor.

Purple juice exploded everywhere.

Silence. Then chaos.

Lila dropped character and howled. "Mom! You look like you lost a fight with a jam factory!"

Zeke peered down at her. "Bea, honey, you're wearin' more fruit than a church social in July."

Marla, trying to stay pristine on a log, smirked—until a squirrel, offended by the commotion, dropped a fir cone squarely on her head. "Ow! This forest is assaulting me!"

Finn zoomed in. "Note the alpha predator asserting dominance via conifer artillery."

Bea sat up slowly, face and hair streaked violet. She looked like a very dignified grape.

She opened her mouth—everyone braced for a lecture—then closed it. A slow grin spread across her berry-stained face.

"Laugh it up, you hyenas," she said, scooping a handful of mashed salmonberry and flinging it at Finn.

Direct hit. Splat on his hoodie.

Finn yelped. "Mom! That's chemical warfare!"

"All's fair in love and re-enactment," Bea deadpanned, lobbing another berry bomb at Zeke, who ducked too late. Zeke retaliated with a muddy handful that caught Marla square in the chest.

Marla gasped like a Victorian lady spotting an ankle. "You. Did. Not."

"Oh, I did," Zeke cackled. "Welcome to the food fight, Princess Priss!"

Marla's eyes narrowed. She scooped mud with surprising speed and nailed Zeke in the ear. "Consider that my resignation from dignity." Within seconds the trail became a battlefield. Berries flew. Mud arced. Lila used the fake chicken as a shield. Finn deployed his phone as a drone (until a berry took it out).

Hologram Ethel flickered into existence on a nearby stump, hands on hips, watching the carnage with pure glee. "Y'all are terrible at historical accuracy," she hollered over the shrieks, "but A+ for enthusiasm! In my day we didn't have salmonberries—we had actual dust! You kids got it easy!"

Bea, now thoroughly purple and grinning like a maniac, yelled back, "Easy? You try raising two of your genetic replicas!"

Ethel pretended to consider. "Fair point. But I did it without Netflix, so we're even."

A particularly enthusiastic mud clod from Lila caught the hologram, passing right through and splattering a fern behind it.

Ethel clutched her chest in mock horror. "Direct hit! I'm dyin'—again!"

Lila bowed. "Grandma, you taught us violence is the sincerest form of flattery."

Eventually, the ammunition ran low, and the combatants collapsed against trees, panting and painted like abstract art. Marla, mud-streaked and breathless, actually laughed—a real one, not her usual polite titter. "I haven't been this filthy since…ever."

Zeke offered her a hand up. "Stick with us, city girl. We'll get you properly ruined by supper."

Bea wiped berry from her eyes and looked around at her ridiculous, filthy, laughing family. She felt something loosen in her chest—something that had been knotted since the day she'd learned neatness was safer than Ethel's brand of joy.

Hologram Ethel gave them a salute. "Scene complete. You pass—barely. Next clue tomorrow at the oyster farm. Bring bibs and bail money."

She vanished with a wink.

Finn checked his cracked phone screen. "We're trending on my imagination. Five stars."

Lila slung an arm around Bea's berry shoulders. "Mom, you're officially too cool for the library now." Bea snorted. "Don't push it. Someone's doing laundry tonight."

But she didn't mean it. Not really.

As they squelched back down the trail—purple, muddy, and bonded in mutual destruction—the rainforest seemed to laugh along with them, dripping approval from every leaf.

Chapter 5: The Great Okie Oyster Ordeal

Low tide at the Tofino Oyster Farm smells like the ocean's armpit—briny, fishy, and unapologetically alive. The Hargroves arrived in a convoy of rubber boots and skepticism, buckets clanking like jailhouse tin cups. The morning mist still clung to the flats, making everything look like a watercolor left out in the rain.

Hologram Ethel was already waiting on the barnacled dock, hip-deep in virtual water, wearing chest waders and a grin sharp enough to shuck with.

"Mornin', ya sorry sack of sea monkeys!" she bellowed over the gulls. "Challenge Five: Harvest the Magic Oysters usin' my Oyster-O-Matic 3000. These ain't ordinary bivalves—these are great-grandbabies of the very clams I traded for gasoline in 1936. Find the ones marked with a red X. Use the machine. Do NOT use dignity—that's contra-band."

The contraption squatted on the dock like a mechanical octopus that had lost a fight with a bicycle shop: pedals, suction hoses, a conveyor belt made from old fan belts, and a dye gun that looked suspiciously like a repurposed Super Soaker.

Marla took one look and recoiled. "I have a shellfish allergy. Also a nonsense allergy. And a smell allergy."

Zeke inhaled deeply. "That's the perfume of profit, princess. Low tide and high chaos—Ethel's signature scent."

Finn circled the machine, geeking out. "Pedal kinetics trigger pneumatic suction, sorts by density, marks with edible dye. Grandma basically invented automation before automation was cool."

Lila vaulted onto the bike seat. "Dibs on propulsion! Let's get shucking!"

Bea raised a cautionary finger. "Safety protocol. No one stands in the—"

Lila pedaled like she was late for the Tour de France.

The Oyster-O-Matic awoke with a death-rattle roar. Hoses plunged into the mud. Oysters rocketed up like salty missiles.

For fifteen beautiful seconds it was poetry: clams clacked along the belt, sorted themselves, and plopped neatly into buckets.

Then came the hiccup.

Pressure spiked.

Then—KA-BLOOEY.

The machine burped a bivalve blizzard.

Oysters launched in every direction with ballistic enthusiasm.

Zeke took one to the forehead with a cartoon THUNK. He staggered back and sat hard in seaweed. "Well, shuck me sideways! I've been personally brined!"

An oyster zipped into Finn's hoodie pocket and began a spirited escape attempt. He froze. "It's alive! It's doing the backstroke in my chest hair!"

Lila, still pedaling, wheezed with laughter. "Finn, you've been molested by a mollusk!"

Marla ducked—and caught a prime specimen right down the front of her borrowed overalls. It slid to a cozy stop. She shrieked a note that scared every gull within a mile. "There is a shellfish in my brassiere!"

Bea dodged left, right—then WHACK, an oyster clipped her ear. "That's battery with intent to garnish!"

Hologram Ethel doubled over cackling. "Y'all move prettier than a cat on a hot tin roof! Reminds me of '36—outside Barstow, runnin' on fumes, three clams in my pocket and a trucker with a leer and no teeth."

The family paused mid-ducking to listen, oysters still pinging off railings like edible hail.

Ethel leaned on her virtual pitchfork. "Truck stop diner. Sign said GAS FOR CASH ONLY. I had no cash, but I had clams I'd dug from a roadside ditch—big juicy ones. Offered 'em to the pump jockey. He laughed till he cried, said, 'Little girl, what am I supposed to do with those?' I said, 'Eat 'em, trade 'em, or propose to 'em—your choice.'"

Zeke, rubbing his forehead, grinned. "You left out the proposal part."

"Didn't leave it out," Ethel shot back. "He proposed right there by pump three. Said he'd fill my tank and throw in a ring if I'd stay. Told him the only ring I wanted was onion-flavored. Took the gas and left him standin' there with three clams and a broken heart."

Lila whooped. "Grandma, you broke men with seafood!"

"Only the ones with no teeth," Ethel said primly. "Standards, sugar. Standards."

The machine, now fully demonic, pivoted and began hosing the dock with a high-velocity oyster fountain.

Marla, still excavating her overalls, shrieked again as another clam pinged off her backside. "I've been goosed by Grandma's ghost gadget!"

"Technically," Finn panted, dodging, "you've been bivalve-slapped."

Bea grabbed a bucket and started catching mid-air like a pro. "If we're harvesting, we're harvesting efficiently! Lila, throttle down! Finn, clear the jam! Zeke—stop flirting with the wildlife!"

Zeke was juggling two oysters like Benihana chef. "These babies got spirit! One just tried to unionize."

Marla, to everyone's shock, cracked an oyster against a piling, slurped it raw, and paused—eyes widening.
"That's...obscenely good."

Ethel clapped. "Atta girl! First one's free, second one costs your soul."

An hour later—dock half-flooded, clothes half-ruined, dignity fully bankrupt—they had a bucket brimming with red-X oysters.

Bea, seaweed in her hair and triumph in her eyes, held up the haul. "We did it. Against all laws of physics and common sense."

Lila slung a salty arm around her mom. "Mom, you're the shuckin' queen. Oyster boss level unlocked."

Finn cradled a perfect specimen. "These are going viral. Or at least viral-adjacent."

Marla licked salt from her fingers. "I hate you all. But I'm keeping these overalls."

Ethel raised her pitchfork in salute. "Challenge cleared. Y'all pass with flying shellfish and a side of sass. Tomorrow's the finale—back at the cabin. Bring glue, duct tape, and your last shred of sanity. We're assemblin' my masterpiece."

She flickered out with a wink, leaving the family knee-deep in mud, laughter echoing across the flats, and the distinct feeling that Ethel Hargrove—even dead—was still winning.

Chapter 6: Cabin Capers and Creative Chaos

The morning of the penultimate challenge dawned clear for once, as if the Pacific Northwest had finally run out of rain and decided to phone it in. The Hargroves gathered in Ethel's cluttered living room, surrounded by decades of half-finished inventions: a wind-powered toaster, a self-rocking chair that had once trapped Zeke for three hours, and enough spare parts to rebuild a small submarine.

Hologram Ethel flickered into existence atop the coffee table, wearing a tool belt stuffed with wrenches and what appeared to be a stick of dynamite (hopefully decorative). She held a rolled-up blueprint the size of a yoga mat.

"Final warm-up, ya magnificent messes!" she announced. "Challenge Six: Assemble my masterpiece—the Hargrove Harmony Engine. It's a Rube Goldberg symphony that waters plants, brews coffee, feeds the birds, and plays 'Waltzing Matilda' on kazoos. All at once. Blueprints are in the box under the couch. Parts are scattered like my good sense—everywhere. You got till sunset. Fail, and I haunt you with polka remixes."

Bea eyed the overflowing box of gears, springs, PVC pipe, and suspiciously sticky glue. "This is impossible. It's a mechanical migraine."

Ethel grinned. "Impossible's just possible's lazy cousin, Beatrice. Get crackin'."

Lila dove in first, emerging with a fistful of sprockets. "This is gonna be epic! Or epically explosive." Finn sorted parts with nerdy precision. "It's a chaotic state machine with deliberate entropy. Grandma invented organized anarchy."

Marla, now permanently in borrowed flannel because her wardrobe had surrendered, picked up a funnel. "If this ends with me glued to anything, I'm billing the afterlife." Zeke rattled a box of marbles. "Relax, darlin'. Worst case, we build a perpetual motion machine that perpetually annoys the neighbors."

They set to work. Or what passed for work.

Lila squeezed super glue onto a gear. Too much. Way too much. The gear bonded instantly to the table. She yanked. The table came with it. "Uh…new design feature?" Bea sighed. "Lila, that's not a feature. That's a furniture felony."

Finn tried to solder a wire and accidentally zapped himself. He hopped around like a caffeinated frog. "Static shock! Grandma booby-trapped the copper!"

Ethel cackled. "Only a little. Builds character. Or third-degree burns."

Zeke, tasked with the kazoo manifold, tested one. It produced a sound like a goose passing a kidney stone. He played a few notes anyway. "I'm callin' this movement 'Ode to Indigestion.'"

Marla, attempting to connect PVC pipes, cross-threaded one. It shot off like a rocket, ricocheting off the ceiling and knocking over a lamp. "This house is trying to kill me! Again!"
"Welcome to the family," Bea deadpanned, catching the pipe mid-air. "Death by DIY is tradition."

Glue mishaps escalated. Finn's hand stuck to a lever. Lever stuck to Zeke's sleeve. Zeke's sleeve stuck to Lila's hair. Lila's hair stuck to Marla's flannel pocket.

They formed an accidental human centipede of craftsmanship.

Finn tugged. "We're a Hargrove chain gang!" Lila laughed so hard she snorted. "More like a sticky situation—glued and screwed!" Marla, face turning red, strained against the bond. "I did not escape Vancouver traffic for arts-and-crafts bondage!"

Zeke wheezed. "Speak for yourself. This is the most action I've had since '89."

Bea surveyed the glued-up conga line and did something unprecedented: she squeezed the glue bottle deliberately, adding another dollop to connect herself to the chain. "If you can't beat 'em," she declared, "join 'em in abject humiliation."

Ethel slow-clapped. "That's my girl! Nothin' says family like involuntary togetherness."

Hours passed in a blur of zingers and disasters.

A spring launched, beaning Finn in the forehead. "I've been sprocket-rocked!" A pulley system collapsed, dumping marbles everywhere. Zeke slipped, arms flailing, and bowled into the others like a geriatric strike. "Spare me the drama!"

Marla, now fully invested despite herself, wrestled a coffee percolator into place. "If this thing doesn't brew perfect espresso after all this, I'm converting to herbal tea and spite."

Lila rerouted a hose that instantly sprayed Zeke in the face. "Baptism by caffeine—consider yourself brewed anew!"

As sunset painted the windows orange, the machine stood finished: a towering, unstable monument to madness, decorated with bird feeders, coffee pots, watering cans, and a kazoo orchestra that seemed like it had been designed by a committee of caffeinated squirrels.

Bea, hands on hips and glue in her hair, flipped the master switch.

Gears turned. Marbles rolled. Water trickled. Coffee dripped. Birds (real ones) swooped in for seed. And finally, gloriously, the kazoos wheezed into a wobbly, off-key "Waltzing Matilda."

The family stood in stunned silence.

Then erupted.

Lila jumped up and down. "We built harmony from havoc! We're chaos virtuosos!"

Finn fist-pumped. "Entropy engineered—patent pending!"

Marla wiped a tear—laughter or glue solvent, unclear. "I hate you all. But that was…magnificent."

Zeke saluted the machine. "Ethel, you beautiful lunatic. You turned us into a functioning disaster."

Hologram Ethel appeared one last time that day, eyes suspiciously shiny.

"Y'all did it," she said softly. "Not the machine. You. You stuck together—literally and otherwise. Tomorrow's the grand finale: Ethel Fest on the beach. Public performance of my life story. Costumes mandatory. Embarrassment guaranteed. Bring everyone. It's time to show the island what Hargroves are made of."

She paused, voice dropping to a whisper only they could hear.

"I'm proud of you knuckleheads. Every sticky, loud, ridiculous one of you."

Then she vanished, leaving the Harmony Engine humming its kazoo lullaby and five glue-flecked, coffee-stained, utterly exhausted Hargroves grinning like fools in the golden light.

They didn't bother cleaning up. Some messes, they were learning, are masterpieces in disguise.

Chapter 7: The Grand Finale Fumble

The day of Ethel Fest broke bright and blustery, the kind of

Vancouver Island weather that can't decide between sunshine

and tantrum. Word had spread through Tofino's grapevine—ferry captains, surf shops, the Coombs goats—until half the west coast seemed to migrate toward Chesterman Beach. Locals brought folding chairs, coolers, and curiosity. Tourists brought phones and confusion. Someone had even strung a banner between drift logs: ETHEL HARGROVE—QUEEN OF CONTROLLED CHAOS, 1917–2025.

The Hargroves stood backstage (a tarp draped over driftwood) in costumes stitched together from thrift-store finds, Ethel's old overalls, and pure desperation. Lila was young Ethel: freckles drawn with eyeliner, straw hat, and a tiny chicken harness. Finn played the Cluck-O-Mobile as a one-man band of pedals and pulleys. Zeke was cast as every grumpy hen and disapproving sheriff. Marla, to her own horror, had been roped into narrating in a posh accent that kept slipping into Canadian apologies. Bea—Bea was the director, script in one hand, kazoo in the other, looking like a woman who'd finally accepted that order and mayhem are just roommates.

The script was simple: a slapstick retelling of Ethel's life, from Dust Bowl exodus to island legend, culminating in the Harmony Engine's kazoo finale. Props included the Rain Repeller, a scaled-down Oyster-O-Matic, and fifty kazoos distributed to the audience "for participation."

Because Ethel had an obsession.

It started, hologram Ethel explained in the pre-show warm-up (projected twenty feet tall above the surf), in the endless Okie nights of 1935.

"Couldn't afford a radio," she drawled to the crowd, larger than life and twice as loud. "Couldn't afford much of anything. But kazoos? You could make one from wax paper and a comb. Cheap, portable, and loud enough to drown out despair. I'd play 'Red River Valley' till the stars got embarrassed. Kept the dust devils dancin' and the loneliness quiet. Turned out, if you kazoo hard enough, the universe has to hum along."

The crowd chuckled. A kid in the front row tested his free kazoo—BRRRRT—and got shushed by his mother.

Ethel winked. "Save it for the finale, sugar. We're goin' symphonic."

The play began.

Lila burst onto the "stage" (packed sand) pedaling Finn's ridiculous contraption while Zeke flapped behind as the hens. The Cluck-O-Mobile wobbled valiantly. A hidden fan blew dust (organic oat flour, for safety) into the air. Lila cracked an imaginary whip. "Mush, you feathered freeloaders!"

A wheel came off. Finn face-planted spectacularly. The audience roared.

Zeke clucked indignantly, then launched into an improvised hen monologue about workers' rights. "We demand shorter treadmills and better seed!"

Marla, narrating from the side, deadpanned, "And lo, the poultry unionized. Management was powerless."

Next scene: the Rain Repeller. Bea activated it proudly. It worked—until Zeke "accidentally" kicked the pressure valve. A gentle mist became a horizontal fire hose. Half the front row got baptized. Screams turned to laughter as people realized it was fresh water.

A surfer in the audience yelled, "Best shower I've had all week!"

Then the Oyster-O-Matic. Lila pedaled. Real oysters (pre-shucked for mercy) flew—into buckets manned by volunteers. One escaped trajectory and landed in Marla's narration script.

She picked it up, glared at the crowd, and slurped it without breaking character.

"Thus," she declared, mouth full, "Ethel sustained herself on grit, gumption, and garnish."

The crowd lost it.

Mid-show, storm clouds rolled in—unscripted, dramatic, perfect. Wind whipped the tarp. Rain threatened.

Bea froze for a heartbeat. Then she grinned exactly like her mother.

"Improv time," she muttered.

They skipped straight to the finale.

The Harmony Engine was wheeled out—larger now, reinforced overnight with community help. Every moving part had a kazoo attached. Fifty of them. Plus the audience's fifty.

Bea raised her conductor's baton (a driftwood stick with a marshmallow on the end).

"On three," she shouted over the wind. "One...two...Ethel!"

She flipped the switch.

Gears turned. Marbles rolled. Coffee brewed (and immediately blew away in the gale). Birdseed scattered. Watering cans sprinkled the front row like holy water.

And the kazoos—oh, the kazoos—erupted into the most gloriously awful rendition of "Waltzing Matilda" ever inflicted on nature.

A hundred voices, zero talent, one heartbeat.

Off-key didn't begin to cover it. It sounded like a bagpipe convention in a blender. Seagulls fled. Dogs howled in sympathy. Children covered their ears and laughed until they fell over.

Zeke led the hen section with enthusiastic clucking. Lila pedaled backup rhythm. Finn's drone (repaired) buzzed overhead, dropping biodegradable confetti. Marla abandoned dignity entirely and conducted the audience with theatrical flair. Bea stood in the center, soaked, wind-whipped, kazoo at her lips, playing louder than anyone.

The rain hit just as the final note wheezed out—a downpour worthy of Ethel's old nemesis.

But nobody ran for cover.

They danced. Slipped. Splashed. Kazooed through the deluge like it was the only sensible response.

Hologram Ethel appeared one last time, life-sized now, standing in the surf as if the ocean itself had invited her.

She didn't speak loudly. She didn't need to.

"Y'all turned my mess into music," she said, her voice echoing over wind and rain. "That's the real inheritance. Not gadgets. Not stories. Just this—laughin' in the rain with people who get your kind of crazy."

She looked straight at Bea.

"I was autistic in a world that didn't have the word yet," she said simply. "Patterns were my friends when people weren't.

Inventions were my voice when words got tangled. Kazoos were my proof that even noise can be harmony if you're brave enough to make it."

The crowd had gone quiet, rain drumming on hoods and hats.

Ethel smiled, soft and fierce.

"Keep makin' noise, family. The world needs more beautiful racket."

She raised her own kazoo—where'd she get that?—and played one clear, perfect note that cut through the storm.

Then she faded, pixel by pixel, into the rain.

The audience erupted—cheers, applause, kazoos blazing a triumphant encore.

Later, when the storm cleared, and the beach looked like a confetti battlefield, the Hargroves scattered Ethel's ashes from the Harmony Engine's birdseed hopper. Gentle. Silly. Perfect.

Bea watched the gray dust swirl into the wind and surf. Finn slung an arm around her. "She'd hate a somber ceremony." "She'd call it a waste of good wind," Bea agreed.

Lila started humming "Waltzing Matilda" off-key. Zeke joined in. Marla—Marla—added harmony. Bea pulled Ethel's original harmonica from her pocket, the one from the goat, and played along.

Five voices, one ridiculous instrument, and the endless Pacific keeping time.

Somewhere in the distance, a lone kazoo answered—carried on the breeze, or maybe just imagination.

Either way, it sounded like laughter.

And that was inheritance enough.

Chapter 8: The Evergreen Echoes

Six months later – July 4, 2026

The summer sun hung low over Chesterman Beach as it had finally decided to stick around for the party. The Hargroves were back on Vancouver Island, not for a funeral this time, but for what Lila had dubbed the First Annual Ethelapalooza.

A hand-painted sign (Lila's handiwork, naturally) leaned against a driftwood log: ETHEL FEST II – NOW WITH 50% LESS RAIN (RESULTS MAY VARY).

The Harmony Engine had been rebuilt bigger, sturdier, and with twice as many kazoos. It now occupied permanent pride of place beside Ethel's cabin, solar-powered and programmed to play a different off-key tune every hour. Locals timed their beach walks to the 3:00 p.m. kazoo rendition of "Sweet Caroline," which had become weirdly addictive.

Bea stood at the grill in Ethel's ancient overalls—patched, faded, and now officially hers—flipping salmon burgers with the calm authority of a woman who had survived oyster artillery and lived to tell the tale. She'd retired from the library for good and taken over Ethel's workshop. Her first invention: a Rain Repeller Mark IV that actually worked without incidental tsunamis. She sold them at the Tofino Saturday market under the brand name "Mostly Dry."

Finn sat cross-legged on the sand, laptop balanced on his knees, demoing his new app to a cluster of curious surfers. It was called Cluck—part augmented-reality treasure hunt, part family-story archive. Users could scan Ethel's old artifacts (now on permanent rotating display in the cabin) and watch holographic snippets of her tall tales. He'd launched it three months ago. It had hit a million downloads last week. He still tripped over his own feet when excited, but now he laughed about it instead of apologizing.

Lila, sun-browned and salt-streaked, led a gaggle of kids in a re-enactment of the Great Oyster Ordeal—using water balloons instead of actual shellfish. She'd turned the beachfront into an eco-art installation: driftwood sculptures wired with solar lights and, of course, kazoos that played whale sounds when the wind blew. Her latest grant proposal? "Mayhem as Environmental Education." It got funded in record time.

Zeke held court under a beach umbrella, taller tales than ever. "And then the oyster hit Marla right in the—" He paused as the woman herself appeared beside him, handing him a cold drink.

Marla—yes, that Marla—now spent half the year in Tofino. She had bought the lot next door, canceled the plans for a McMansion, and built a tiny cedar studio instead. She claimed it was for "wellness retreats," but everyone knew she just wanted to be near the chaos. She still wore cashmere, but now it was cashmere that had survived mud fights and kazoo symphonies. She even started a podcast: City Mouse, Country Mayhem. Episode 12: "I Was Pearl-Necklaced by a Ghost."

The Harmony Engine hit four o'clock and wheezed out a shaky "Oh Susanna." Dozens of people—locals, visitors, new friends—pulled kazoos from their pockets and joined in. The sound was still awful. But it was perfect.

Bea looked up from the grill, spatula paused mid-flip. For a moment she thought she saw her—a flicker in the corner of her eye: Ethel in overalls, leaning against the cabin porch rail, arms crossed, grinning like she'd planned every second of this.

Bea raised her kazoo in salute.

The flicker smiled back and was gone.

Later, as the sun dipped into the Pacific and the bonfire crackled loudly, the family gathered around the Harmony

Engine one last time that night. Finn had added a new feature: a small projector hidden in the bird feeder.

He pressed a button.

A life-sized hologram of Ethel appeared—not the scripted challenge version, but a quiet recording no one had seen before. She sat on the porch steps in her favorite rocking chair, with the evening light softly illuminating her face.

"Hey, ya glorious disasters," she said, voice gentle. "If you're watchin' this, you did it. You kept the noise goin'. That's all I ever wanted. Not perfection. Not money. Just you lot— laughin', inventin', lovin' each other loud enough to scare the quiet away."

She paused, looked straight into the camera—straight at them.

Bea, honey, stop tryin' to organize the chaos in life. Finn, finish what you start—even if it blows up. Lila, focus that wildfire heart of yours; it's gonna light up the world. Zeke, keep lyin'—the truth's boring anyway. And Marla…welcome home, sugar. Took you long enough.

Soft chuckle.

I was different, y'know. My brain was wired like a pinball machine during a lightning storm. The world didn't always understand me. But I found my people. And now you've found yours. Keep adding to the tribe. Keep making beautiful noise.

She lifted her battered harmonica—the original, from the goat—and played a slow, sweet verse of "Red River Valley." Clear notes, no wobble.

When the last note faded, she smiled one last time.

"See you in the wind, the rain, and every off-key kazoo. Love you bigger than the Dust Bowl sky."

The hologram winked out.

Silence held for a heartbeat.

Then Lila started humming the tune. Finn joined in on kazoo. Zeke added harmonica. Marla—voice cracking just a little—sang the words. Bea closed her eyes and let the music wrap around her like the island mist.

Around them, the bonfire popped, waves rolled in, and a hundred kazoos—carried by friends new and old—rose in answer.

The noise was glorious.

Somewhere, Ethel Hargrove was laughing her Okie laugh, boots kicked up on the porch of whatever came next, satisfied at last.

The mayhem, it turned out, was eternal.

And that was the best inheritance of all.

===

Chapter 9: The Unexpected Sequel – Return of the Cluck

July 4, 2027 – One Year After Ethelapalooza II

The beach was packed tighter than a Tofino parking lot in whale-watching season. Ethelapalooza III had outgrown Chesterman Beach and spilled onto Mackenzie Beach next door. There were food trucks selling "Ethel's Okie Tacos," a kazoo flash-mob, and a sanctioned re-enactment of the Great Oyster Ordeal using foam balls (the local oyster farmers had politely but firmly requested no more live ammunition).

Bea—now officially "Bea the Builder" to the island kids—stood on a makeshift stage beside the third-generation Harmony Engine, which had grown into a solar-powered monstrosity the size of a small food booth. It brewed coffee, dispensed free sunscreen, watered a vertical herb garden, and still played hourly kazoo concerts. She wore Ethel's overalls like a uniform now, patches added for every new disaster survived.

Finn's Cluck app had exploded into a full platform; people worldwide were uploading their own family mayhem stories, complete with AR holograms. He'd hired a small team and moved into a converted shipping container office behind the cabin. He still tripped over cables daily, but now he live-streamed it for content.

Lila's eco-art had gone viral—literally. One of her driftwood-kazoo whale sculptures had been installed in Vancouver's airport, where it played whale songs in 12-part disharmony. She'd also started dating a marine biologist who thought controlled chaos was a valid research method.

Marla's podcast had hit the top 100. She now splits her time between Tofino and Vancouver, hosting sold-out "Mayhem Mindfulness" retreats where city dwellers pay good money to get muddy and kazoo-bombed.

Zeke, ninety-three and counting, had become the unofficial mayor of mischief. He rode around on a mobility scooter decorated with chicken feathers and a custom horn that played "Waltzing Matilda."

Everything was perfect.

Which, of course, meant it was time for Ethel to ruin it.

At exactly 3:00 p.m.—the traditional kazoo hour—the Harmony Engine did not play "Sweet Caroline."

Instead, every speaker on the beach crackled. Every phone running the Cluck app pinged. The giant projector screen (donated by a tech-bro fan) flickered to life.

And there she was.

Hologram Ethel. Again.

New outfit: aviator goggles, a leather jacket that definitely hadn't existed in her wardrobe, and a smirk sharp enough to cut rebar.

The crowd went silent except for one confused tourist who whispered, "Is this part of the show?"

Ethel surveyed the masses like a general eyeing conquered territory.

"Well, slap my pixels and call me a glitch!" she boomed. "Look at this circus! Y'all took my little shindig and turned it into Woodstock for weirdos. I'm prouder than a peacock in a mirror factory."

Bea dropped her spatula. "Mother?!"

Finn's jaw hit the sand. "That's impossible. The hologram files were archived. The projector's offline except for scheduled—"

Ethel waved a dismissive hand. "Boy, I built self-replicating code before you built your first Lego. You think I wouldn't leave a back door?"

Lila squealed. "Grandma's back!"

Marla muttered, "I need a stronger drink."

Zeke cackled so hard his scooter backfired.

Ethel continued. "Now, I was plannin' to rest in peace—honest—but then I saw what y'all did with my legacy—turned it into a franchise! Merch! Podcasts! A bloody app! I ain't mad. I'm flattered. But also…bored."

She leaned forward conspiratorially.

So I wrote myself a sequel. One more challenge. Bigger. Louder. Global.

The screen split. A new app icon appeared: CLUCK 2.0 – THE GREAT GLOBAL GOOSE CHASE.

"Rules are simple," Ethel said. "I hid fifty golden kazoo eggs—actual gold-plated kazoos—all over the world. Each one triggers a new hologram story from my life that nobody's heard yet. Find 'em all, piece together the secret grand finale invention, and you win…well, you'll see."

She grinned wickedly.

The first clue drops in exactly one hour. Teams of five. No cheating—except the fun kind. Loser has to host next year's Ethelapalooza in…Oklahoma.

The crowd gasped. Oklahoma in July? Cruel and unusual.

Bea found her voice. "Mother, you can't just hijack our festival from beyond the grave—again!"

Ethel winked. "Watch me, sugar. One more ride. For old times' sake. And because eternity's long, and I missed y'all's beautiful racket."

She paused, softer now.

Besides… there's one story I never told you. The real reason I left Oklahoma. The one that don't fit on a kazoo.

The hologram flickered, almost shy.

Help me tell it properly.

Then she vanished.

The beach erupted—cheers, groans, frantic downloading of the new app update.

Bea observed her family: Finn frantically coding, Lila bouncing like a pogo stick, Marla resignedly booking plane tickets, Zeke revving his scooter like a race car.

She sighed, picked up her spatula, and flipped another salmon burger.

"Fine," she said to the sky. "One more rodeo."

Somewhere in the cloud—whether literal or figurative—Ethel Hargrove chuckled her signature Okie laugh, boots kicked up on a server rack in the afterlife, ready to drag her family (and half the world) into fresh chaos.

The golden kazoo hunt was on.

And the evergreen echoes just got a whole lot louder.

Chapter 10: The Golden Hum – Ethel's Oklahoma Secret

August 15, 2027 – Somewhere above the Atlantic

The Hargrove jet (chartered, not owned—Finn's app money stretched far, but not that far) hummed at 35,000 feet. Bea sat buckled in, staring at the Cluck 2.0 app on her tablet. The first golden kazoo had been found two weeks ago in Paris by a team of French bakers who thought it was performance art. The second surfaced in Tokyo, discovered by a street musician who immediately incorporated it into a viral kazoo-metal fusion video.

Now the third clue had dropped, pointed squarely at Oklahoma.

The app notification pinged in Ethel's voice: "Head to the Panhandle, ya jet-settin' jackrabbits. Place where the dirt was blackest and my heart was heaviest. Look for the windmill that still turns when there ain't no wind. Clue's in the blades."

Bea's stomach knotted. She hadn't been back to Oklahoma since Ethel's funeral in '85.

Lila, sprawled across two seats with noise-canceling headphones blaring kazoo covers of sea shanties, sat up. "We're really going there? Grandma's origin story?"

Finn, typing furiously, nodded. "Coordinates point to the old Jenkins homestead. Or what's left of it. Satellite shows a single windmill still standing."

Marla sipped champagne and grimaced. "Dust Bowl tourism. How…rustic."

Zeke, upgraded to first class and loving it, raised his plastic cup. "Back to where it all began. Ethel's gonna spill the beans she buried deeper than oil."

They landed in Amarillo under a sky so wide it felt accusatory. Rented a dusty SUV and drove northwest until pavement gave way to caliche roads and memories.

The Jenkins place was a ghost: foundation stones, a collapsed barn, and one lone Aermotor windmill creaking in a breeze that wasn't there. Its blades turned slowly and steadily, powered by something hidden.

Finn's drone confirmed it: a small solar motor Ethel must have installed decades ago, keeping the blades moving long after the well ran dry.

They climbed the tower carefully—rust flaked like dead skin. At the top, wedged between two blades, was the golden kazoo: polished brass plated in real gold, engraved with tiny chickens marching in a circle.

Lila carefully extracted it. The moment her fingers closed around it, the kazoo warmed. A faint projector beam shot from the mouthpiece, casting a hologram against the vast Oklahoma sky.

Ethel appeared—not the cackling chaos queen, but younger. Eighteen. Dust in her hair, with eyes older than her years. She stood in front of the same windmill, 1935, as a black blizzard rolled in behind her like a wall of night.

"This is the one I never told," she said quietly. "The real reason I left."

The family stood transfixed as young Ethel spoke.

My baby sister Ruthie was six. Sweetest thing—autistic like me, but softer. Didn't talk much, but she saw patterns in everything. Clouds, stars, the way dust drifted. One storm came worse than the rest. Black as sin, thick as tar. We hunkered in the root cellar. When it passed…Ruthie was gone. Wandered out lookin' for the pattern in the storm, they said. Found her two days later under a drift, curled up like she was sleepin'. Holdin' a kazoo I'd made her from a comb and tissue paper.

Ethel's voice cracked—the only time they'd ever heard it.

"I couldn't stay. Every gust of wind sounded like her hummin'. So I built the Cluck-O-Mobile and ran. Told myself I was chasin' rain, but really I was runnin' from silence."

She looked straight into the camera—straight at them, ninety-two years later.

"But I carried her with me. Every invention, every loud contraption, every damn kazoo symphony—it was me keepin' her music alive. Keepin' the quiet from winnin'."

Older Ethel flickered in beside her younger self, translucent, smiling through tears.

"The secret wasn't shame, darlin's. It was love. Too big for one lifetime. So I spread it across the world in golden eggs for you to find. Each kazoo holds a piece of Ruthie's song. Collect 'em all, and the final invention plays it complete—for everyone."

Young Ethel lifted her kazoo and played a simple, haunting melody—five notes, repeating like a lullaby.

Older Ethel joined in harmony.

Then both vanished.

The windmill blades slowed to a stop.

Lila was crying openly. Finn's glasses were fogged. Marla stared at the horizon like she'd been punched in the soul. Zeke removed his hat.

Bea clutched the golden kazoo to her chest.

"She never told me," she whispered. "All those years."

The kazoo vibrated gently. A new notification appeared on their phones—Ethel's voice, soft now.

"Next clue: Head north to where the northern lights dance with prairie fire. Look for the aurora kazoo under the midnight sun. But take your time, sugars. Some songs are meant to be chased slow."

The screen faded to a single line:

For Ruthie. Keep humming.

They stood on the windmill platform a long time, five silhouettes against the endless Oklahoma sky, listening to the creak of old metal and the whisper of wind that sounded— almost—like a child humming through wax paper and comb.

The hunt was no longer just mayhem.

It was a lullaby, golden and scattered, waiting to be made whole.

And the Hargroves—louder, messier, and more loving than ever—were going to sing it back to the world.

Chapter 11: Black Blizzard Lullaby

April 14, 1935 – Reconstructed, Oklahoma Panhandle

The golden kazoo's hologram didn't fade this time. It held.

The windmill platform dissolved into pixels, and suddenly the Hargroves stood in 1935.

Not virtually—viscerally.

The air turned thick, gritty, metallic. Daylight vanished as a wall of black earth rolled toward them from the north, a living mountain of dust two miles high. The temperature dropped twenty degrees in seconds. Static crackled in their hair.

Young Ethel—eighteen, rail-thin, freckles lost under grime—stood with them now, real enough to touch. She clutched a tiny hand: Ruthie, six years old, red curls tangled, eyes wide and fixed on the approaching storm like it was a kaleidoscope only she could read.

The family felt it in their bones—the terror of a sky turning to soil.

Bea's throat closed. She had read about Black Sunday, the worst storm of the decade, but reading wasn't this: the suffocating weight, the taste of dirt on the tongue, the way sound itself was swallowed.

Ethel spoke without looking away from the storm.

"April 14. They called it Black Sunday after. Worst one yet. We'd had rollers all week, but this…this one ate the sun."

Ruthie tugged her sleeve. "It's pretty, Ethel. Look—the swirls match the wallpaper pattern Mama burned last winter."

Ethel's smile was brittle. "Yeah, baby. Real pretty. Time to go downstairs now."

But Ruthie didn't move. She tilted her head, listening to something none of them could hear.

Bea stepped forward instinctively, reaching for the child who looked so much like childhood photos of her own mother. "Ruthie, honey, come with us."

Ruthie turned. Her eyes—Ethel's eyes—met Bea's with unnerving directness.

"You're from the loud place," she said softly. "The place with all the kazoos."

Bea's heart cracked open.

The storm hit.

Day became night in a heartbeat. Wind screamed like a freight train. Dust blasted through every seam of the farmhouse below them. The hologram showed it all: plates rattling off shelves, curtains billowing inward like ghosts, the single lightbulb swinging wildly.

Down in the root cellar, the family huddled—Ma clutching a Bible, Pa coughing blood into a rag, Zeke (barely twenty) holding a lantern with shaking hands.

Ethel tried to pull Ruthie down the stairs.

But Ruthie slipped free.

"I need to see the end of the pattern," she whispered, and darted up into the black.

Ethel's scream was raw, animal. "Ruthie!"

The hologram froze on that moment—Ethel lunging after her sister, dust swallowing them both.

Present-day Ethel appeared beside them, older, translucent, tears cutting clean tracks through the simulated dust on her cheeks.

"I chased her for hours after the storm passed," she said, voice rough. "Found her two miles away, under a drift taller than the barn. Curled up like she'd just laid down for a nap. Still holdin' that little wax-paper kazoo."

She reached out as if to touch Ruthie's frozen image.

"I built every loud, ridiculous thing after that to fill the quiet she left. The Cluck-O-Mobile wasn't an escape—it was a search. Every mile, I was lookin' for her in the wind."

Lila was sobbing openly now, arms wrapped around herself. Finn's face was wet, glasses fogged beyond use. Marla—stoic, unflappable Marla—had both hands over her mouth. Zeke's shoulders shook silently.

Bea stepped through the dust to her mother.

"Why didn't you ever tell me?"

Ethel met her eyes, fierce and broken.

"Because some hurts are too big for words, baby. I thought if I kept 'em buried, they couldn't bury you too. But Ruthie…she deserved better than silence."

The storm began to ease in the hologram—dust settling, a blood-red sun peeking through.

Young Ethel knelt in the snowbank, holding Ruthie's small body close. She placed the wax-paper kazoo to her lips and played those same five notes—soft, steady, unwavering.

The melody rose through the devastation like a thread of light.

Older Ethel joined in now, golden kazoo in hand. Then the present-day family—hesitant, voices cracking—added their harmony.

Five notes, repeating.

A lullaby against the end of the world.

When the last note faded, the hologram shifted one final time.

Ruthie—small, translucent now—stood beside her older sister. She smiled, shy and radiant, and reached out to touch each of them: Bea's cheek, Lila's curls, Finn's hand, Marla's trembling fingers, Zeke's weathered knuckles.

"Thank you for finding my song," she whispered.

Then she placed her tiny wax-paper kazoo into Bea's palm.

The vision dissolved.

They were back on the windmill in 2027, sunset bleeding across the quiet plains.

The golden kazoo in Lila's hand glowed softly. A new message etched itself into the metal:

Next stop: Reykjavik. Under the aurora where fire meets ice. Bring the lullaby. Ruthie wants to dance.

Bea gripped the wax paper relic—fragile and irreplaceable.

The windmill creaked once, as if sighing.

Far off, a dust devil spun up briefly—small, harmless—then unraveled into clear sky.

Bea looked at her family, eyes red but steady.

"We're not just chasing kazoos anymore," she said. "We're bringing her home."

No one argued.

They climbed down the windmill in silence, carrying two kazoos now—one gold, one paper—and a melody heavy enough to anchor the sky.

The Black Blizzard was long gone.

But its lullaby had only just begun to travel the world.

Chapter 12: The Symphony of Scattered Souls

November 22, 2027 – Reykjavik, Iceland, Under the Aurora

The northern lights danced overhead as Ruthie's patterns came to life—swirls of emerald and violet weaving through the ink-black sky, chasing each other in silent chaos. The Hargroves stood on a frozen lava field, breath fogging in the sub-zero air, the final golden kazoo clutched in Bea's gloved hand. It had taken them three months to chase the last one here: under a geothermal hot spring in Iceland, where fire met ice in a hiss of steam and stone.

They'd collected all fifty now—scattered from the Eiffel Tower's shadow to Tokyo's neon alleys, from the Amazon's canopy to this frozen edge of the world. Each kazoo unlocked a fragment of Ruthie's lullaby, a new verse in Ethel's untold story: how autism had been their secret language, a world of hyper-focused wonders amid the Dust Bowl's despair.

Ruthie saw symphonies in dust motes; Ethel built machines to play them. The world called them "odd," "distant," "broken." Ethel called it power.

"Neurodiversity ain't a flaw," her hologram had said in a Sydney clue, projected against the Opera House sails. "It's evolution's wildcard. Ruthie didn't talk much 'cause words were too blunt for her colors. I invented 'cause patterns screamed to be shaped. We weren't wrong—we were wired for wonders the 'normals' couldn't dream."

In Cape Town, another fragment: "Isolation hurt worst. Folks stared, whispered. But in our heads? Fireworks. Ruthie'd flap her hands to match the storm's rhythm; I'd rig a windmill to hum her tune. Autism wasn't the enemy—the silence was."

Bea turned the final kazoo over in her palm. It pulsed with warmth, all fifty now resonating in the backpack at her feet—like a choir tuning up.

"Ready?" she asked.

The family nodded, faces illuminated by the aurora glow. Lila's eyes sparkled with unshed tears; Finn adjusted his glasses, fingers trembling not from cold; Marla gripped Zeke's arm; Zeke hummed softly, off-key but steady.

Bea placed the last kazoo into the makeshift stand they'd built—a portable Harmony Engine 5.0, engineered by Finn with global crowd-sourced tweaks. It looked like Ethel's original, but amplified: solar panels for power and wireless sync with the Cluck app worldwide.

She flipped the switch.

The machine hummed. Then sang.

Fifty golden kazoos vibrated in unison, playing Ruthie's lullaby—complete now, a five-note motif blooming into a symphony. Layers unfolded: dust swirls in counterpoint, chicken clucks as percussion, rain patters as melody. It wasn't pretty. It was raw, discordant, beautiful—like autism itself, a pattern too vast for neurotypical ears.

Holograms erupted around them: Ethel and Ruthie, life-sized, dancing under the aurora. Young Ethel twirled her sister, laughing as Ruthie flapped her hands to match the lights' rhythm.

The app broadcast it live. Millions tuned in—families like theirs, neurodiverse souls who'd joined the hunt, sharing stories of their own "odd" wiring turned to wonder.

Ethel's voice overlaid the music, her final message.

"We assumed we were broken 'cause the world said so. But look—Ruthie's pattern was the storm's gift, my inventions its echo. Autism ain't a cage; it's a lens: sharper focus, deeper dives, wilder creations. The 'mayhem' was our way of shoutin' back at the quiet. Don't hide your wiring, darlin's. Rewire the world instead."

Ruthie's hologram looked out at them—at everyone watching.

"Keep humming," she whispered. "The patterns need you."

The symphony crested, aurora pulsing in sync, then faded to a single, lingering note.

Silence fell, profound and peaceful.

Bea wiped her eyes. "She did it. She turned pain into this."

Lila hugged her. "We all did."

The northern lights flared brighter, as if applauding.

Epilogue: Eternal Echoes

2035 – Vancouver Island, Ethel Hargrove Neurodiversity Center

The cabin had grown into a campus: workshops buzzing with inventors, gardens patterned like Ruthie's dust swirls, a kazoo amphitheater where families gathered to "make racket" against isolation. Bea, now eighty, ran it all—her "Mostly Dry" inventions funding scholarships for autistic creators worldwide.

Finn's Cluck empire had pivoted to neurotech: apps that translated sensory overload into art, turning "flaws" into features. Lila's eco-sculptures dotted the globe, each humming Ruthie's lullaby on wind-powered kazoos. Marla's retreats healed thousands, blending mindfulness with mayhem. Zeke, a hundred and one, still told tales from his scooter, now with holographic Ethel as backup.

On the anniversary of the symphony, they gathered on Chesterman Beach. The Harmony Engine—global now, with nodes on every continent—played the lullaby at midnight.

Bea stood in the surf, wax-paper kazoo in hand.

Mother, Aunt Ruthie—you taught us the powerful truth: Autism isn't a puzzle to solve; it's a perspective to embrace. In a world of silence and sameness, be the noise. Be the pattern that breaks the mold. Turn your 'different' into defiance, your focus into fire. The quiet may come, but the hum—the beautiful, chaotic hum—endures.

She played the five notes.

The world hummed back—millions of kazoos, from Reykjavik to Oklahoma, joining in digital harmony.

Ethel's laugh echoed on the wind.

The mayhem wasn't over.

It was just beginning.

Made in the USA
Coppell, TX
19 January 2026

68481014R10073